THE GOLDEN SPIKE

HOW A PHOTOGRAPH CELEBRATED THE TRANSCONTINENTAL RAILROAD

by Don Nardo

Content Adviser: Bob Zeller
Co-Founder and President
The Center for Civil War Photography

COMPASS POINT BOOKS
a capstone imprint

Compass Point Books are published by Capstone,
1710 Roe Crest Drive, North Mankato, Minnesota 56003
www.capstonepub.com

Editor: Catherine Neitge
Designer: Tracy Davies McCabe
Media Researcher: Wanda Winch
Library Consultant: Kathleen Baxter
Production Specialist: Charmaine Whitman

Image Credits
Bridgeman Images: ©Museum of the City of New York, USA/Frances Flora Bond
(Fanny) Palmer, 17, 56 (top), Peter Newark American Pictures/Private Collection,
30; Capstone, 31; Courtesy of the family of Andrew J. Russell, 34, 59 (left); Getty
Images: MPI, 24; Library of Congress: Prints and Photographs Division/Alfred A.
Hart, 42, Andrew J. Russell, 5, 7, 26, 33, 36, 51 (all), 54, 57 (bottom), 59 (right),
Anthony Berger, 21, 56 (b), John Carbutt, 23; National Archives and Records
Administration, cover, 13, 19, 44, 48, 58; North Wind Picture Archives, 18, 57
(t); The Cooper Collection of U.S. Railroad History, 45, 47; Union Pacific Museum
Collection: C. Everett Johnson, 22, Andrew J. Russell, 43; Yale Collection of American
Literature, Beinecke Rare Book and Manuscript Library, Andrew J. Russell, 11, 15, 25,
27, 28, 39, 40, 53

Library of Congress Cataloging-in-Publication Data
Nardo, Don, 1947–
The golden spike : how a photograph celebrated a connected continent / by
Don Nardo.
pages cm.—(Compass point books. Captured history)
Summary: "Chronicles the historic meeting of two railroad lines in 1869 that
linked the U.S. transcontinental railroad and Andrew J. Russell's famous
photograph of the event"—Provided by publisher.
Includes bibliographical references and index.
ISBN 978-0-7565-4991-6 (library binding)
ISBN 978-0-7565-4997-8 (paperback)
ISBN 978-0-7565-4999-2 (ebook PDF)
1. Pacific railroads—History—Juvenile literature. 2. Railroads—United States—
History—Juvenile literature. 3. Railroads—West (U.S.)—History—Juvenile
literature. I. Title.
TF25.P23N37 2015
385.0973'09034—dc23   2014036134

Printed in the United States of America in North Mankato, Minnesota.
092014   008482CGS15

TABLEOFCONTENTS

ChapterOne
HISTORIC CONNECTION

Andrew J. Russell stood near a tall tree towering by itself in a canyon in the northern reaches of the Utah Territory. Standing beside the Union Pacific Railroad's still unfinished new line, the aged pine marked the spot at which the tracks had come exactly 1,000 miles (1,609 kilometers). Company employees wanted to commemorate making it that far from Omaha, in Nebraska Territory, where construction had begun four years before. They made a sign that read "1000 Mile Tree" and hung it from the lowest branch of the pine.

A group of about 40 Union Pacific workers posed beneath the tree on January 9, 1869. One of them had climbed to the top. At the right moment, Russell signaled him to wave, and, with a camera mounted on a tripod, he captured the scene. A photographer who had made a name for himself creating visual images of the recently fought Civil War, Russell, 39, had been hired the year before by the Union Pacific. His assignment was to document one of the largest construction projects ever attempted in the United States.

In 1862 Congress had passed legislation authorizing the creation of the first transcontinental railroad, which would link the eastern United States to the West Coast. Some far-thinking people had been calling for such a project for almost 20 years. Yet at the time Congress

His assignment was to document one of the largest construction projects ever attempted in the United States.

A railroad worker perches atop the 1000 Mile Tree in Andrew Russell's 1869 photo. The Weber Canyon, Utah, tree has since died, but was replaced by a new pine tree.

approved it, not all Americans saw the wisdom of it. A few even thought that building a railway line more than 1,700 miles (2,736 km) long through vast stretches of largely unexplored wilderness was impossible. They continued to echo the sentiment of a Cincinnati newspaper that had ridiculed the idea. To claim that the railroad link would "create settlements, commerce and wealth," the 1846 article said, was like pledging "to unite neighboring planets in our solar system and make them better acquainted with each other."

But the naysayers began to fall silent as the gigantic project slowly but steadily moved forward. In the mid-1860s, as the Union Pacific headed westward from Omaha, another company—the Central Pacific Railroad Company—pushed eastward from California. Their goal was to meet somewhere in between, forming a single railway line that would bridge much of the continent. Early in 1869 it became clear that the historic meeting place would be in northern Utah.

After getting his shot of the workers and the ancient tree in early January, Russell moved on. He and his three assistants, including Stephen Sedgwick, a young man with a keen interest in history, did their best to keep up with the railroad crews. The Union Pacific's foremen and their many workers moved along at a furious pace, often laying down 4 miles (6.4 km) or more of track in a day.

Russell and his aides had to take photos of more than the work itself. They were also expected to photograph the towns and scenic wonders through which the railway line passed. That required them to travel back, forth, and sideways along the route, looking for and documenting whatever Russell thought was most significant.

In the 1860s taking photos, especially outdoors, was a slow, painstaking procedure. Including the processing phase, taking a single shot could consume two hours or more. So it was not unusual for Russell to fall behind the work crews, forcing him to catch up on his way to another camera setup. Usually he had no idea what his next subject

In the 1860s taking photos, especially outdoors, was a slow, painstaking procedure.

Railroad workers in 1868 remove rock and soil, called digging out a cut, in Echo Canyon, Utah.

would be, so he rarely could plan ahead very far.

One major exception loomed on the horizon, however. Now that the Union Pacific tracks were nearing the spot where they would connect with those of the Central Pacific, he needed to plan. The ceremony marking the event was expected to engage a worldwide audience, and he would be one of only a handful of photographers present. To maintain his reputation, he needed to be as organized and otherwise prepared as possible.

It would have been far easier for Russell to do his job if he could have traveled light. But that was impossible for him, as it had been for Mathew Brady and the other well-known Civil War photographers. The typical equipment they carried included a box camera weighing up to 30 pounds (14 kilograms), a second device called a stereo camera because it captured two images at the same time, a collection of delicate glass plates and lenses, many bottles of chemicals for sensitizing the glass plates and developing the photos, and a tent that could be a mobile darkroom. All of this equipment, some of it fragile, had to be carried by wagon. And that slowed Russell and his assistants considerably, particularly in the rugged terrain through which the railway passed.

Russell and other photographers of the times employed a complex and very time-consuming method of creating pictures. "Wet-plate process" was only one of its many names. The photographer first cut a glass plate into the desired size. Often it was 10 by 13 inches (25 by 33 centimeters), but there were several other sizes. He or she then mixed chemicals and carefully poured a sticky mixture of collodion onto one side of the plate. The photographer then went into what was called a darkroom, even though for field photographers the "room" was often a black tent or a wagon.

In the darkroom the photographer sensitized the plate in a bath of silver nitrate for several minutes before placing it in a lightproof wooden plate holder. The next steps were to insert the plate holder into a slot in the camera box and, while the plate was still wet, to aim the camera at the scene to be photographed. Then the

Railroad foreman Jack Casement walks by Russell's field darkroom wagon near the tracks in Utah.

photographer removed a dark slide from the plate holder to expose the plate to the still-covered camera lens. There was no shutter, so the photographer took off the lens cap to expose the plate to the light for several seconds. The photographer then replaced the lens cap, reinserted the dark slide, removed the plate holder, and took it inside the dark tent or wagon. He or she then took the plate out of the holder and developed it in the dim orange light coming through the small "safe light" window in the tent.

Despite the difficulties and awkwardness of photography at the time, everyone involved agreed that it had to be used to document the historic venture. And in addition to the historical significance of the railroad photos, there was money to be made when photographers sold their images. It was becoming obvious that simple words and drawings were no longer enough to portray major news events. The photographic medium, which had been invented earlier in the century, also had to play its part. In 1867, two years before the completion of the first transcontinental railroad, a Philadelphia magazine declared, "Nothing seems beyond the reach of photography. It is the railway and the telegraph of art. The telegraph detects and catches the thief, and so does photography. The railways carry us to points afar, and so does photography—[in fact] it does more."

As late as March 1869, no meeting place had been established. So the two track-laying operations kept going. Finally they passed right by each other in the Utah wilderness. (Both companies made a lot of money for each mile of track they laid. So their directors decided to keep construction going until Congress chose the place where the two lines of track would connect.) In the words of Grenville M. Dodge, the Union Pacific's chief engineer, the two lines were now "running side by side, and in some places one line was [on a raised embankment] right above the other."

Because of the closeness of the two lines, the tens of thousands of workers involved—along with their tents, wagons, animals, and equipment—covered several square miles. For a distance of 30 miles (48 km) to the west of the small town of Corinne, Utah, the *Salt Lake Deseret News*

It was becoming obvious that simple words and drawings were no longer enough to portray major news events.

THE RAILROAD AND AMERICAN INDIANS

Russell photographed Shoshone Indians who had given the Union Pacific right of way to land in Wyoming.

As the Union Pacific wound its way westward in the 1860s, it helped to bring more and more whites into the Indian-inhabited lands lying west of the Mississippi River. It disrupted and forever changed the way American Indians had lived for thousands of years.

At first Plains tribes mostly left the railroad workers alone. But a series of battles between U.S. soldiers and Plains tribes began in the mid-1860s. And as the railroad pushed westward, warriors harassed the railroad workers. Small groups of Sioux and Cheyenne raided work sites and stole horses, cows, and other livestock. They also killed some railroad surveyors who had pushed ahead of the work crews to scout out the best routes for the tracks.

In the meantime, the Union Pacific had a tribal ally—the Pawnee—who were bitter enemies of the Sioux. The company often hired Pawnee men for protection against other tribes. In return, the railroad allowed Pawnee people to ride the work trains for free. Also, in October 1866, company executives hired some Pawnee to stage a mock raid on a train to entertain politicians and other dignitaries riding inside.

ChapterTwo
IMMENSE UNDERTAKING

The building of the first transcontinental railroad across North America was one of the largest and most challenging construction projects of the modern era. Many people took part in making it a reality. Among others, they included three U.S. presidents; hundreds of congressmen and senators; hundreds more railroad executives, surveyors, engineers, and telegraph operators; and tens of thousands of laborers.

But in measuring the contributions of individuals to the project's image in history, few matched those of a single gifted man—Andrew Russell. As the Union Pacific's official photographer, he documented the building of the railroad in a large collection of visual images. Because of their power, Americans then—like Americans ever since—were impressed by the scale and splendor of the project. Russell also gave posterity the most familiar and widely circulated image associated with the transcontinental railroad. Taken immediately after the completion of the great undertaking, the picture affirmed that railroads were the most advanced form of transportation on Earth.

Considering both the grand railroad project and Russell's involvement in it, the world-famous photo was more than two decades in the making. In 1840, when Russell was 11 years old, few people could have envisioned any sort of transportation network in the vast lands lying

The bridge over Dale Creek in Wyoming has been called one of the greatest engineering feats of the 19th century. It was the longest and highest bridge on the Union Pacific Railroad.

beyond the Mississippi and Missouri river systems. This was largely because of the region's remoteness.

In those days most Americans probably shared the view of an Army explorer, Stephen Harriman Long. In 1820 he led an expedition across the Plains to the Rocky Mountains. Long thought the area was dry and desolate and called it a great American desert. It was "almost wholly unfit for cultivation," he said, "and of course uninhabitable by a people depending upon agriculture for their subsistence." These words, which turned out to be misleading, discouraged settlement of the region for a generation.

By the 1840s, however, attitudes about the West had begun to change. Explorers and settlers reported that the region contained many valuable natural resources and large tracts of land that could be farmed. Influential writers declared that the resources and potential farmland belonged to the American people. John O'Sullivan, the editor of the popular *United States Magazine and Democratic Review*, famously summed up this view in 1845. God, he wrote, had intended that the western frontier be exploited by the United States. "Our manifest destiny," he said, is "to overspread the continent allotted by Providence [God] for the free development of our yearly multiplying millions."

Many writers, politicians, and other Americans began using the term O'Sullivan had coined, "manifest destiny." They spread the idea that God wanted the United States to absorb the rest of the continent. This would naturally require a transportation network to connect the West to the East, and O'Sullivan was an early backer of the idea of building a transcontinental railroad.

The need for such a railroad linkage came to the fore again only three years later, in 1848, when gold was found in California. The discovery set in motion the famous gold rush, in which thousands of would-be prospectors journeyed to California.

They spread the idea that God wanted the United States to absorb the rest of the continent.

Manifest destiny was expressed artistically in Fanny Palmer's 1868 lithograph, *Across the Continent: Westward the Course of Empire Takes Its Way.*

Some easterners who hoped to strike it rich braved the six-month overland trek across the continent. Others boarded ships and sailed around Cape Horn, at South America's southern tip, which also took up to six months or more. A second sea route—by way of the Isthmus of Panama—was several months faster, but the trip was much more expensive. The Panama Canal did not yet exist. So the Pacific Mail Steamship Company took

Gold seekers bound for California faced expensive, months-long journeys west.

passengers from the U.S. East Coast to eastern Panama. They went through the jungle-covered isthmus on foot or in wagons, then boarded another of the company's ships for the rest of the trip to California.

In the 1850s matters related to North versus South came to overshadow those dealing with East and West. During that turbulent decade, several northern politicians advocated building an intercontinental railroad to link the towns and cities of the East to the Pacific coast. The trains that took that route, they said, would carry more than just travelers. They would also haul settlers and the

Survey teams started planning potential railroad routes in the 1850s.

construction materials they needed to reshape the western plains and mountains.

But the federal legislation needed to make such a project a reality was repeatedly blocked. The main reason was that most southern leaders, landowners, and merchants were opposed to creating a cross-country railway line. They pointed out that the departure point for every projected westward route was located in either a northern state or a territory far from the South. Such a situation would exclude southern access to the railroad, they claimed. It would also make it easier for the North to fill the western territories with settlers who opposed slavery.

The opposition to building a transcontinental railroad almost entirely disappeared when southern states left the Union, bringing on the Civil War. Most members of Congress were Republicans, as was President Abraham Lincoln. They were willing to back him in practically any project that might expand the Union and make it stronger. Lincoln felt that a transcontinental railroad would do that. His opinion mirrored that of a railroad executive who said such a project would be "a means of holding the Pacific Coast to the Union." Author Barry B. Combs points out that it "required the dissolution of the Union to clear the way for the project."

With plenty of support in Congress for the new railroad, the Pacific Railway Act passed on July 1, 1862. It provided huge land grants and the government bonds

The opposition to building a transcontinental railroad almost entirely disappeared when southern states left the Union, bringing on the Civil War.

needed to borrow money to build a transcontinental line. The plan was for construction crews of the Central Pacific Railroad company to begin in California and head east, and for those of the Union Pacific company to start in the Midwest and move westward.

The Union Pacific's energetic main boss, Thomas Durant, was determined to make his company's part of the venture a success. So he hired a highly experienced

Grenville Dodge (right) met Abraham Lincoln by chance in Council Bluffs, Iowa, in 1859. Lincoln, who was running for president, asked the young engineer what would be the best railroad route west. "From this town out the Platte Valley," Dodge replied. And that's the route it would take, starting across the Missouri River in Omaha.

civil engineer, Grenville M. Dodge, to head his team of engineers. (Dodge and other railroad engineers were experts in the planning, grading, and construction of railway lines and bridges, as opposed to locomotive engineers, who drove the trains.)

The multitalented Dodge had spent much of the 1850s doing surveying work for railroad companies

DURANT'S HUGE SCAM

Doc Durant posed for a photographer using a stereo camera when the tracks reached the 100th meridian October 6, 1866, near Cozad, Nebraska.

Thomas C. "Doc" Durant, the executive in charge of the Union Pacific Railroad in the late 1860s, claimed to be an honest businessman. But he was anything but honest. Behind the scenes he profited from scams and other shady dealings for most of his adult life. He made millions during the Civil War, for instance, smuggling illegal shipments of cotton from the Confederacy to the North.

Durant also benefited handsomely from schemes involving railroad companies. The most audacious and famous of these swindles caused a scandal called the Crédit Mobilier affair. In the mid-1860s Durant set up the Crédit Mobilier company. His plan was for it to become the construction company that would build the transcontinental railroad. Because Durant headed both the Union Pacific and Crédit Mobilier, he was essentially hiring himself to construct the railroad line.

Here's how the scam worked: Crédit Mobilier presented the Union Pacific with bills for its construction work. The bills included what Crédit Mobilier actually spent on materials and workers plus the company's fee. The Union Pacific then passed the bills on to the government, adding its own fee in the process. So when the government paid the bills, Durant and his cronies pocketed all the money the companies made except for the basic costs. A New York City newspaper, *The Sun*, revealed the Crédit Mobilier scheme to the public in 1872. The ensuing scandal ruined the careers of several politicians who had invested money in the companies. But the slippery Durant managed to go largely unpunished. He kept the money he had made in the scam, although he did lose a big chunk of it in an international financial crisis the following year, the Panic of 1873.

General Grenville Dodge served with distinction during the Civil War.

and later became a Union army general. He and Durant were nothing alike. "Durant was everything the serious engineer was not," Combs notes. He was "a flashy dresser, sharp-tempered, [and] completely knowledgeable in the shifting money market of the immediate post-war years."

The Union Pacific broke ground in Omaha in December 1863. But it would be nearly two years before construction would begin.

He provided "the political favors to make the building of the railroad possible." Dodge, meanwhile, "supplied the drive, the organizational ability and technical skill that got the job done in the face of overwhelming physical problems."

The job did not take long to get under way. President Lincoln announced the location of the Union Pacific's starting point on November 17, 1863. He said the city of Omaha, in Nebraska Territory, would be "the point from which the line of railroad and telegraph" would begin its westward journey. It was an immense undertaking in that era. Dodge later provided a short summary of

the number of workers and pack animals required, along with the tremendous challenges involved in the transport of supplies, materials, and equipment: "At one time we were using at least 10,000 animals, and most of the time from 8,000 to 10,000 laborers. The bridge gangs always worked from five to twenty miles ahead of the track, and it was seldom that the track waited for a bridge. To supply one mile of track with material and supplies required about forty [train] cars, as on the plains everything—rails,

Castle Rock looms over railroad workers as they build temporary and permanent bridges across Wyoming's Green River. Russell called the famous landmark Citadel Rock in the caption for his photo.

A supply train is unloaded at the end of a track near Fort Bridger, in Wyoming.

ties, bridging, fastenings, all railway supplies, fuel for locomotives and trains, and supplies for men and animals on the entire work [project], had to be transported from the Missouri River."

The railroad foremen, known as bosses, who directly oversaw the workers, were demanding and often gruff. They regularly pushed the laborers hard, at times at a grueling pace, to ensure that a certain amount of track would be laid each day. That instilled both respect

Dan Casement (in the doorway) is flanked by his clerks in Echo City, Utah. Dan handled payroll and accounting while his brother Jack directed track construction.

and even touches of fear and awe in the workers. Two prominent Union Pacific bosses, brothers Dan and Jack Casement, were small men. But as Combs says, "the men who worked for them would swear the Casement boys were seven feet tall and tough as nails."

Under the bosses' constantly watchful eyes, the workers toiled, usually 12 or more hours a day, seven days a week, with only an occasional weekend off. The work was highly regimented and very hard. English traveler

Day after day, week after week, Andrew Russell continued to compile his visual account of the giant project.

W.A. Bell, who watched the Union Pacific operation for several days in 1866, described it. The track-laying was "a science," he wrote. "A light [rail] car, drawn by a single horse, gallops up to the front with its load of rails. Two men seize the end of the rail and start forward, the rest of the gang taking hold by twos until it is clear of the car. They come forward at a run. At the word of command the rail is dropped in its place, right side up, with care, while the same process goes on at the other side of the car. Less than thirty seconds to a rail for each gang, and so four rails go down in a minute! … There are ten spikes to a rail, four hundred rails to a mile, eighteen hundred miles to San Francisco. … Twenty-one million times are those sledges [hammers] to be swung—twenty-one million times are they to come down with their sharp punctuation, before the great work of modern America is complete!"

Even as eyewitnesses such as Bell wrote descriptions of the construction process, a different, more powerful sort of documentation was also under way. Day after day, week after week, Andrew Russell continued to compile his visual account of the giant project.

It had not been by mere chance that he had landed this choice position with the Union Pacific. Company officials, some of whom had served in the Civil War, were well aware of the way that conflict had been visually documented by skilled photographers, notably Mathew Brady, Alexander Gardner, Timothy O'Sullivan, and Russell himself. The executives reasoned that their

Jack Casement's crew laid track, pausing only briefly for the photographer.

railroad project must also be captured in photos. After all, Durant publicly stated, the massive undertaking was seen by many as "the great work of the age." Yet it was not simply because of the venture's historical significance that they wanted it to be preserved in photos. Even more important to them was the value such pictures would have in exciting the imaginations and gaining the support of investors and politicians, not to mention the American public.

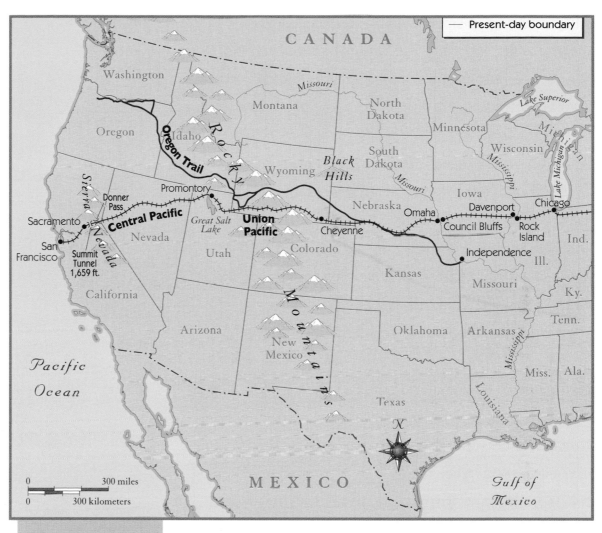

The railroad's route stretched across the western U.S.

In 1868, therefore, Durant hired Russell to document the Union Pacific's role in the creation of the first transcontinental railroad line. Because the project had begun well before he was hired, Russell had to catch up with the company's operation. His work began at Cheyenne, in southeastern Wyoming.

In a sense, Russell felt, he had been preparing for this important assignment all his life. He was born March 20, 1829, in Walpole, New Hampshire, the son of Joseph Russell and Harriet Robinson Russell. When Andrew was still young, the family moved to Nunda, New York, where the boy took a keen interest in painting and drawing. His talents were strong enough for him to be hired to create several portraits in his hometown when he was a teenager. During the same years, Russell developed a fascination with trains and railroads that would later serve him well.

In October 1850, at age 21, Russell married Catherine Adelia Duryee, and the couple had two daughters, Cora and Harriet. Little is known for certain about Russell's family life. But it appears to have been troubled, because within a few years his wife and daughters were living apart from him. Part of the problem may have been that he tended to immerse himself completely in his work and other activities, leaving little time for his family.

In one such activity, in 1861, Russell helped to recruit Union soldiers for the Civil War effort. He joined the army himself in 1862, receiving the rank of captain in the 141st New York Infantry Regiment. Early in 1863 he studied photography with independent photographer Egbert Guy Fowx, who sold images to both the army and the renowned New York photographer Mathew Brady.

Soon afterward, in March 1863, Russell became the official photographer for the United States Military Railroads unit. General Herman Haupt, who commanded the unit, "authorized the extensive distribution of Russell's work," says Bob Zeller, an expert on Civil War photography. "By mid-February 1864, more than 6,500 large photographs and 368 small photographs had been

He tended to immerse himself completely in his work and other activities, leaving little time for his family.

Russell photographed his Army commander, General Herman Haupt, paddling a small raft. The craft was built for scouting operations in the Civil War.

distributed to President Lincoln and sixty-seven others in the administration or the military."

Most of Russell's war photos showed railroad-related objects and activities. But now and then he had the chance to photograph scenes of combat. "On one occasion," Zeller wrote in his book, *The Blue and Gray in Black and White: A History of Civil War Photography*, "Russell was so close to enemy soldiers he could see—and photograph—their faces."

The only known
photograph of
Andrew Russell

By the close of the war in 1865 Russell had become, in Combs' words, "a supreme technician" of the art of photography. "For negative quality and reproduction of detail, his photographs were unsurpassed by any photographer of his day." This explains why the Union Pacific executives were so eager to hire him to be the company's chief photographer.

Once he began the assignment, Russell photographed

> **"When he saw a strong picture possibility, he took several shots, each with a slightly different viewpoint."**

as many aspects of the transcontinental Union Pacific operation as possible. He often took pictures at random, shooting whenever a promising subject presented itself. He reasoned that the diverse images could be sorted through and edited later. In his mind, maximum coverage was vital because it was a once-in-a-lifetime historic series of events. "As the steel rails raced to infinity," wrote researcher Karen Current, "pushing the untouched land before them like glacial fingers, Russell and his photographic assistants logged the miles on their glass plates." She said he "chronicled as much as his camera could encompass. When he saw a strong picture possibility, he took several shots, each with a slightly different viewpoint." He decided later which viewpoint was best because "the particular moments of the history-making event would not be repeated."

To Russell, it was not just the building of the railroad in the midst of the western wilderness that was history-making. The images he captured of the wilderness itself would be no less momentous and fascinating to millions of Americans. It must be remembered that he was one of the first photographers to take a camera into the vast landscape beyond the Nebraska and Kansas plains.

Most people who lived in the East and Midwest had never traveled to those distant regions. So Russell gave them their first look at the West's rugged mountain ranges, deep forests, and huge stretches of arid desert. The preface to an 1869 collection of his photos aptly

Russell featured a photo of Castle Rock in his 1869 book,
The Great West Illustrated in a Series of Photographic Views.

summarized his goal, which he achieved remarkably well. His pictures of the American West, it said, were "calculated to interest all classes of people, and to excite the admiration of all reflecting minds as the colossal grandeur of the Agricultural, Mineral, and Commercial resources of the West are brought to view."

In addition, Russell knew well in advance that he would be providing Americans as well as the citizens of foreign lands with a visual slice of history. Eventually the railway line constructed by his employer, the Union Pacific, would join the line created by the Central Pacific. On that day, he knew, people across the globe would be eager to see a glimpse of the noteworthy event and the formal ceremony celebrating it. Yet there was something even more significant that he could not foresee. It was that one of the photos he would take that day would acquire everlasting fame and would overshadow all of his other pictures. That iconic image would capture the moment when, for good or ill, manifest destiny would become living reality.

ChapterThree
UNITING THE REPUBLIC

The joining of the two railway lines and the gala ceremony marking the historic event had been scheduled to take place at Promontory Summit on May 8, 1869. But the day before, heavy rains caused a flash flood about 50 miles (80 km) to the southeast. The swirling waters damaged a railroad bridge, temporarily holding up a train carrying Thomas Durant and other Union Pacific executives. At the same time, 400 Union Pacific workers refused to allow Durant to go any farther until they received several months of back pay he owed them. Durant got the money and paid them. But because of the time it took to get the money and the time needed for the bridge repairs, the ceremony at Promontory had to be postponed until May 10.

When the big day came, three professional photographers were present. Besides Andrew Russell, representing the Union Pacific, and Alfred Hart, working for the Central Pacific, there was British-born Charles R. Savage from Salt Lake City. Union Pacific engineer Silas Seymour had invited the Mormon photographer to document the historic event.

Russell, Hart, and Savage busied themselves preparing for the camera work to come. As they did so, they saw more and more people arriving, some in train coaches and others by wagon and horseback. Among them were

Russell returned to Utah in the fall to photograph three locomotives testing the new Devil's Gate Bridge. The first temporary bridge across the Weber River had been damaged, delaying the arrival of Durant and other officials at Promontory.

railroad officials, several invited guests, newspaper reporters from nearby towns as well as the East and West coasts, a few railroad workers who were there to lay the last two rails, and a handful of curious citizens from the nearby towns of Ogden and Corinne. Also present that day were more than 200 soldiers and two bands, one from Salt Lake City and the other from Utah's Fort Douglas.

Later estimates of the total number of spectators gathered for the ceremony vary widely, and the actual

Union Pacific officials pose in front of engine *No. 119.*

figure remains unknown. But as National Park Service historian Robert L. Spude points out, "reporters for the *Deseret News* of Salt Lake City, the *Corinne Reporter*, and others generally agree to a little over 1,000" in attendance.

As the crowd grew throughout the morning, the three photographers set up their cameras. They centered their view on a small gap the workers had left between the ends of the two railway lines. This gap was set to be filled

When the final rails were laid, they would be symbolically anchored by a golden spike.

with two connecting rails just before the beginning of the ceremony. When the final rails were laid, they would be symbolically anchored by a golden spike. It and a few other specially made spikes would not be forcefully driven in like ordinary spikes. Instead, railroad executives would lightly tap gold and silver spikes into holes prepared for them. After the ceremony the special spikes would be removed and workers would drive in ordinary spikes to secure the rails.

Drilling the holes for the special spikes was only part of the last-minute preparations. The engineers who drove two huge locomotives—the Central Pacific's *Jupiter* and the Union Pacific's *No. 119*—slowly moved the engines toward the gap in the tracks. They stopped when the trains were facing each other about 70 or 80 feet (21 or 24 m) apart. The plan was for the ceremony to take place on the tracks between them.

At the same time, several telegraph operators were making their own special preparations. Headed by Watson N. Shilling, they added the final touches to a mechanical arrangement that was very high-tech for its time. A telegraphic signal would be broadcast to millions of people across the country signifying the symbolic insertion of the ceremonial spikes. In the weeks just before the big day, telegraph lines had been installed beside the tracks at Promontory. These connected with telegraph offices in Omaha, Chicago, and New York in the East and San Francisco in the West.

In the morning of May 10, operators double-checked a special spike and hammer that already had been wired and attached to the telegraph line. According to the plan, when the hammer touched the golden spike, an electrical signal carrying the code for the letters D O N E would race eastward and westward. It would tell the rest of humanity that the long anticipated transcontinental railroad line had finally become a reality.

As the preparations were going on, Russell and the

Telegraph operators climbed poles to protect the wire from the crowds milling around the ceremony site. The image is one half of a stereograph— photos taken with a stereo camera.

Russell scratched the words "Chinese laying last rail" on his glass plate negative. The Chinese laborers worked for the Central Pacific.

other photographers roamed the site, taking shot after shot of people milling about. Then in late morning, shortly before the ceremony's official opening, a group of workers laid a special commemorative railroad tie made of laurel wood. They placed it beside ordinary pine ones in the gap in the tracks. Then they laid the last two metal rail sections across the ties. (The laurel wood tie would be removed after the ceremony and replaced with a pine tie.)

The wood-burning *Jupiter* (left) and the coal-burning *No. 119* flank the participants in the golden spike ceremony. The telegraph operator's table is below the tracks, to the right.

After the last rails were laid, at a few minutes before noon, the day's formalities finally began. After a minister said a prayer, the emcee, Sacramento banker Edgar Mills, who represented the Central Pacific, announced a series of officials and speakers. Some of them presented ceremonial spikes, one at a time, to Central Pacific official Leland Stanford and other notables. Stanford, a former governor of California, said a few words on behalf of his company.

The Union Pacific's Thomas Durant had planned to speak next, but he was suffering from a splitting headache, so Grenville Dodge spoke in his place.

The golden spike is on display at the Cantor Arts Center at Stanford University. Because the ceremony was postponed by two days, the date inscribed on the spike is wrong.

Finally came the exciting climax of the ceremony, in which company officials would tap the special spikes. Russell and Savage readied themselves in preplanned positions about 100 feet (30 m) from the tracks while Hart perched on the *Jupiter*. At this critical point, the lead telegraph operator, Shilling, sent a message to all the stations in the nationwide hookup. "All ready now," he signaled. "The spike will soon be driven."

Then someone handed Stanford or Dodge the wired hammer. Because the gathered witnesses happened to be strung out along the tracks, very few of them were close enough to see exactly what happened next. Russell and the other photographers also were too far away, and they never got close-up shots of this part of the proceedings. So conflicting reports emerged about who used the hammer first and which spikes they tapped in.

It appears that Stanford was supposed to take care of the golden spike marking the climax of the festivities. According to some sources, he fumbled with the hammer and missed the spike. Other reports claim that, despite his headache, Durant tried his hand and also missed, while still others make no mention of his taking part. In whatever way the events occurred, at 12:47 p.m. local time, Shilling allowed the electrical circuit to close, sending the word "DONE" to the outside world.

As cannons fired and bells pealed in faraway places across the country, at Promontory Summit the crowd issued a huge, joyful shout. A *New York Times* reporter who was present cited "the deafening shouts of the multitude." In the midst of the merriment, the locomotive engineers slowly inched their engines toward each other until their fronts touched. Then the two men climbed down, and each broke a bottle of champagne on the other's locomotive. In the meantime, Russell, Hart, and Savage began taking big, posed shots of the celebration.

It was during the post-ceremony gaiety that Russell took one of the most important photos of the 19th century and probably the most famous railroad image of all time. Its official title is "East and West Shaking Hands at the Laying of Last Rail." But people often call it "East and West" for short. It shows the two locomotives—*Jupiter* and *No. 119*—facing each other about 50 to 60 feet (15 to 18 m) from the camera. More than 100 men, some from the Union Pacific and the others from the Central Pacific, stand in front of their engines. All face the camera.

In the very middle of the shot, Dodge shakes hands with his counterpart, the Central Pacific's chief engineer, Samuel S. Montague. About 20 feet (6 m) behind them, workers standing atop the locomotives hold out champagne bottles to one another. This element of the photo gave rise to its alternate and often-used nickname— "The Champagne Photo."

The image was immediately popular. As Russell

> Russell took one of the most important photos of the 19th century and probably the most famous railroad image of all time.

CHARLES SAVAGE'S BIG DAY

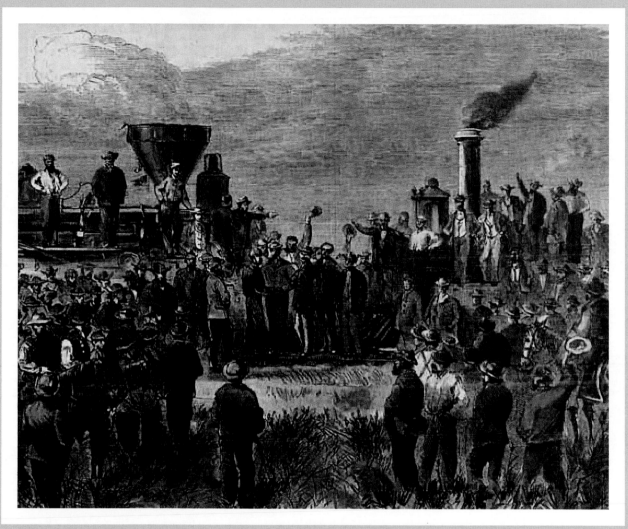

Charles Savage's photograph was the basis for a woodcut that appeared in Harper's Weekly *in June 1869.*

The Salt Lake City photographer, Charles R. Savage, took some excellent photos of the ceremony on May 10, and he also contributed a description of the weather at Promontory Summit on the historic day. He wrote in his diary that he had worked extremely hard all day and had "secured some nice views of the scenes connected with the laying of the last rail. ... Everything passed off lively and the weather was delightful. Saw but little of the actual driving of the Gold Spike and laying of the laurel tie—as I was very busy."

After taking his photos, Savage decided to celebrate what had been a very big day for him. His diary entry reads: "Left the Promontory at five and reached Ogden at 10 o'clock. Cracked champagne with [a friend] and others at West Hotel, where I stayed for the night."

received more and more compliments for it, he recognized its power and importance. "The great railroad problem of the age is now solved," he wrote in *Frank Leslie's Illustrated Newspaper*, where his images appeared as woodcuts. "The continental iron band now permanently unites the distant portions of the Republic and opens up to commerce, navigation, and enterprise the vast unpeopled plains and lofty mountain ranges that divide the East from the West."

Railroad officials do not appear in Russell's most famous photo. It's the workers and engineers who celebrate. The chief engineers, Samuel S. Montague of the Central Pacific (left) and Grenville Dodge of the Union Pacific, shake hands in the center.

1. Samuel S. Montague, Central Pacific chief engineer
2. Grenville M. Dodge, Union Pacific chief engineer
3. James Strobridge, CP construction superintendent
4. George Booth, *Jupiter* engineer
5. Sam Bradford, *No. 119* engineer
6. Elias Jensen
7. John Wilson Kellogg
8. Thomas Shore Wadsworth
9. William Daley
10. Cyrus Arnold Sweet
11. H.L. Harry Greensides
12. Horatio H. Hancock
13. Hezikiah Bissell
14. George Checketts
15. Moroni Strubel Poulter
16. Samuel Faddis
17. (unknown) Hirch
18. Israel Hunsaker
19. Abraham Hunsaker
20. Joshua Williams
21. William Neeley
22. Robert Todd
23. Andrew N. Bjerregard
24. Richard Brown
25. John Percival
26. John Rixon Moseley
27. Joseph Wayment
28. Michael Stanton

ChapterFour
A CHANGING COUNTRY

Large celebrations erupted all across the United States when word was received that the transcontinental railroad had been completed. In Philadelphia officials rang the Liberty Bell, and in San Francisco 220 cannons blasted away. "It was said that more cannons were fired in celebration," historian Stephen Ambrose notes, "than ever took part in the Battle of Gettysburg." Other festivities included a miles-long parade in Chicago, many fireworks displays, and church services from coast to coast.

There is no evidence that Andrew Russell took part in any celebration. He was busy making prints from the plates he had exposed at the ceremony.

Russell's large plate images were for purchase by newspapers to use as the basis for woodcuts, for display in frames, or for publishing in books. He also took hundreds of stereographic images, just as he had during the Civil War. A stereograph is a set of two images exposed at the same time and taken of the same subject slightly apart. The prints were mounted on a holder called a card. The cards were then viewed with a special viewer containing a lens that magnified them slightly. The end product was an image that seemed to be in three dimensions.

Photography expert Bob Zeller calls the 3-D photos the "video" of the Civil War and the West. "It was a much more intimate and complex way of seeing a photo that

The subject of Russell's stereograph—snow sheds—was underlined on the back of the stereo card. When seen through a viewer, the scene looks 3-D. It is one of hundreds of stereo views Russell made in the West.

was wildly popular throughout the second half of the 19th century." He said it was more exciting for viewers than simply seeing a photo.

The stereographs by Russell and others were among the first numbered collectible card series issued in the United States. Zeller said they were some of the "first forms of mass-marketed home entertainment."

After the ceremony at Promontory, Russell continued his work for the Union Pacific. He roamed across California, Utah, and other western states, leisurely taking pictures of scenic landscapes and frontier towns lying near the transcontinental railway line.

51

While Russell was finishing his work for the Union Pacific late in 1869, a volume of his prints was published in New York. Its title was *The Great West Illustrated in a Series of Photographic Views Across the Continent Taken Along the Line of the Union Pacific Railroad West From Omaha, Nebraska.* The front cover of the book had a much simpler title: *Union Pacific Railroad Photographical Illustrations.* Russell also sold his popular stereographs.

In 1870 Russell traveled to New York City, where he remained for the rest of his life. Most of his negatives were acquired by Stephen Sedgwick, who had assisted him with the Union Pacific work. Sedgwick had become a lecturer on the geography and history of the American West. He was happy to use many of Russell's images in his presentations, projecting them on a screen for his audiences.

Sedgwick also sold several collections of the photos, giving them titles such as "Across the Continent" and "Scenes from the Union Pacific Railroad." It is unclear how much money Russell made from the sale of his Union Pacific photos. But historians of photography think it was not much. Today most of the roughly 650 glass plates he created for the railroad are in the Oakland Museum of California. Many of Russell's stereo images are on file at the Library of Congress.

When he moved to New York, Russell worked for *Frank Leslie's Illustrated Newspaper* and set up a photography studio on Logan Street in Brooklyn. He made a modest living at best. He died in relative obscurity September 20,

Russell's photo, "On the Mountains of Green River," appeared in his book, *The Great West Illustrated in a Series of Photographic Views.*

1902, in Brooklyn and was buried in Cypress Hills Cemetery, also in the New York City borough. He was 73.

During Russell's later years, the great project he had visually documented began to change the country in many ways. After the two lines of track converged at Promontory Summit in 1869, settlement of the American West accelerated. It no longer took six months or more to travel from the East to California. Travelers could make the trip in a week.

TRUE SENSE OF VASTNESS

In the caption for his photo of Hanging Rock at the foot of Utah's Echo Canyon, Russell wrote: "From its top can be viewed some of the grandest scenery on the road."

One reason Andrew Russell did such a good job documenting the building of the transcontinental railroad is that he and those behind the monumental project had something important in common. He and the railroad companies both struck out into the vast unknown territories that at the time stretched far beyond the horizons of most Americans. Both the railroad's steel rails and Russell's photos drew the horizons a lot nearer. They brought Americans closer to the still largely unexplored plains, rivers, and mountains of the continent's deep interior.

Russell "carried his camera into an unknown land among widely divergent people and conditions," researcher Karen Current writes. "He had little in the way of tradition or historical precedent to follow." Yet he "had an uncanny ability to depict scale. As few others could, he transmitted a true sense of the vastness of the West and the feeling of space that unfailingly impressed those who traversed that land."

Russell did not foresee that his photos, particularly "East and West," would be widely admired and studied in what was for him the remotely distant 21st century. Yet over time some of the pictures came to be used in many ways, both commercial and artistic. Some have appeared in illustrations for travel guides, and one was used in an ad for a fertilizer company. Countless glass plates, photographic images, and engravings based on them have been displayed in books, magazines, and museum exhibits, and on Internet websites.

The continued popularity of Russell's Union Pacific photos is partly the result of many Americans' fascination with railroads. Even more Americans are still smitten by the allure of the old West and its place in the building of the country. The transcontinental railroad, Russell, his photos, and the vibrant imagery they captured played major roles in an immense drama, author Barry Combs suggests. The stirring pageant was the opening of "the last frontier." The mighty railroad and Russell's photos helped to write "the first chapter of a work that could have only one end" in the long post-Civil War era. It was, Combs says, "the final settlement and form of the United States as one undivided nation."

Timeline

1820

American explorer Stephen Harriman Long leads an expedition into the little-known lands of the far West

March 20, 1829

Andrew J. Russell is born in Walpole, New Hampshire

1845

Newspaper editor John O'Sullivan coins the term "manifest destiny"

1850

At age 21, Russell marries Catherine Adelia Duryee

1860

Abraham Lincoln is elected as the 16th president of the United States

1848

Gold is discovered in California, setting in motion a great 1849 gold rush

1861

The U.S. Civil War begins; Russell helps to recruit Union soldiers

1862

The U.S. Congress passes the Pacific Railway Act, authorizing the building of a transcontinental railroad; Russell joins the Union army

Timeline

1863

President Lincoln announces that the Union Pacific will start its westward journey in Omaha, in Nebraska Territory; the Central Pacific spikes its first rails in California

1865

The Civil War ends; President Lincoln is assassinated; the Union Pacific spikes its first rails in Omaha

April 10, 1869

Congress picks the spot where the Union Pacific and Central Pacific will meet—Promontory Summit in northern Utah

May 10, 1869

The two railway lines come together at Promontory; Russell and two others photograph the festivities

1868

The Union Pacific hires Russell to photographically document its track-laying operation

January 9, 1869

The Union Pacific reaches the 1,000-mile (1,609-km) mark since leaving Omaha

1870

Russell returns to New York City and settles in Brooklyn

September 20, 1902

Russell dies in Brooklyn at age 73

Glossary

commemorative—honoring the memory of something or someone

iconic—famous or instantly recognizable

isthmus—a narrow strip of land that has water on both sides and connects two larger sections of land

locomotive—engine used to push or pull railroad cars

negative—photographic image; areas that are light in the original subject are dark in a negative and those that are dark are light; prints can be made from negatives

posterity—future ages and generations

prints—paper versions of photographs that can be handled or framed

stereo camera—twin-lens camera that takes two almost-identical, side-by-side images at the same time; the two images appear as a single three-dimensional image when viewed together with a stereo viewer

transcontinental—crossing a continent

Additional Resources

Further Reading

Durbin, William. *Until the Last Spike: The Journal of Sean Sullivan, a Transcontinental Railroad Worker, Nebraska and Points West, 1867.*
New York: Scholastic Paperbacks, 2013.

Stein, R. Conrad. *The Incredible Transcontinental Railroad.*
Berkeley Heights, N.J.: Enslow Publishers, 2012.

Uschan, Michael V. *The Transcontinental Railroad.*
Detroit: Lucent Books, 2009.

Willumson, Glenn. *Iron Muse: Photographing the Transcontinental Railroad.*
Berkeley: University of California Press, 2013.

Internet Sites

Use FactHound to find Internet sites related to this book. All of the sites on FactHound have been researched by our staff.

Here's all you do:
Visit *www.facthound.com*
Type in this code: 9780756549916

Critical Thinking Using the Common Core

Photography has changed significantly since the late 1800s when Andrew Russell was taking photos. What are the major differences between early photography's and today's methods? (Key Ideas and Details)

The photo of Andrew Russell on page 34 is the only one known to have survived to the present. From what you have learned about him, do you think he avoided having his picture taken? Why do you think there are no other known photos of him? (Integration of Knowledge and Ideas)

What does "manifest destiny" mean? How did it affect the American Indians living in the West? Did the people behind the transcontinental railroad care about the people already living in its path? (Integration of Knowledge and Ideas)

Source Notes

Page 5, line 7: Edward Rothstein. "The Transcontinental Railroad as the Internet of 1869." *The New York Times*. 11 Dec. 1999. 23 Sept. 2014. http://www.nytimes.com/1999/12/11/arts/the-transcontinental-railroad-as-the-internet-of-1869.html?pagewanted=all&src=pm

Page 10, line 8: Edward L. Wilson, ed. *Philadelphia Photographer*. Vol. IV. Philadelphia: Benerman & Wilson, Publishers, 1867, p 105. https://archive.org/details/philadelphiaphot1867phil

Page 10, line 21: Grenville M. Dodge. *How We Built the Union Pacific Railway And Other Railway Papers and Addresses*. Council Bluffs, Iowa: The Monarch Printing Co., 1910, p. 29. https://openlibrary.org/books/OL7217215M/How_we_built_the_Union_Pacific_railway

Page 12, line 1: Stephen E. Ambrose. *Nothing Like It in the World: The Men Who Built the Transcontinental Railroad, 1863–1869*. New York: Simon and Schuster, 2000, p. 337.

Page 12, line 7: Ibid.

Page 15, line 7: Edwin James. *Account of an Expedition from Pittsburgh to the Rocky Mountains, Performed in the Years 1819, 1820*. Vol. 3. London: Longman, Hurst, Rees, Orme, and Brown, 1823, p. 236. http://content.wisconsinhistory.org/cdm/ref/collection/aj/id/17659/show/17309

Page 16, line 14: John O'Sullivan. "Annexation." *United States Magazine and Democratic Review*, Vol. 17, No. 1. July-August 1845, p. 5. http://web.grinnell.edu/courses/HIS/f01/HIS202-01/Documents/OSullivan.html

Page 20, line 22: *How We Built the Pacific Union Railway and Other Railway Papers and Addresses*, p. 10.

Page 20, line 24: Barry B. Combs. *Westward to Promontory: Building the Union Pacific Across the Plains and Mountains*. Palo Alto, Calif.: American West Pub. Co., 1969, p. 12.

Page 24, line 2: Ibid, pp. 14-15.

Page 25, line 9: *How We Built the Pacific Union Railway and Other Railway Papers and Addresses*, p. 12.

Page 26, line 3: Ibid, p. 16.

Page 28, line 3: *Westward to Promontory: Building the Union Pacific Across the Plains and Mountains*, p. 50.

Page 29, line 3: William A. Bell. *New Tracks in North America: A Journal of Travel and Adventure Whilst Engaged in a Survey for a Southern Railroad to the Pacific During 1867/68*. Vol. II. London: Chapman and Hall, 1869, pp. 254–255. https://archive.org/details/mobot31753000322963

Page 30, line 3: *Westward to Promontory: Building the Union Pacific Across the Plains and Mountains*, p. 17.

Page 32, line 25: Bob Zeller. *The Blue and Gray in Black and White: A History of Civil War Photography*. Westport, Conn.: Praeger, 2005, p. 90.

Page 33, line 5: Ibid, p. 91.

Page 34, line 2: *Westward to Promontory: Building the Union Pacific Across the Plains and Mountains*, p. 16.

Page 35, line 7: Current, Karen. *Photography and the Old West*. New York: H.N. Abrams, 1978, p. 133.

Page 36, line 3: Andrew J. Russell. *The Great West Illustrated in a Series of Photographic Views Across the Continent Taken Along the Line of the Union Pacific Railroad, West from Omaha*. New York: Union Pacific Railroad Company, 1869, Preface. http://brbl-dl.library.yale.edu/pdfgen/exportPDF.php?bibid=2006876&solrid=3434854

Page 40, line 2: Robert L. Spude. *A History of the Site Where the Central Pacific and Union Pacific Railroads Joined to Form the First Transcontinental Railroad, 1869*. National Park Service, 2005, p. 204. http://www.nps.gov/history/history/online_books/gosp1/promontory_summit.pdf

Page 45, line 10: *Nothing Like It in the World: The Men Who Built the Transcontinental Railroad, 1863–1869*, p. 366.

Page 46, line 4: *A History of the Site Where the Central Pacific and Union Pacific Railroads Joined to Form the First Transcontinental Railroad, 1869*, p. ii.

Page 47, col. 1, line 6: Nelson B. Wadsworth. *Set Stone, Fixed in Glass: The Mormons, the West, and Their Photographers*. Salt Lake City: Signature Books, 1996, p. 87. http://signaturebookslibrary.org/?p=21285

Page 48, line 2: John Gruber. "In Light of Promontory." *The Railroad Never Sleeps: 24 Hours in the Life of Modern Railroading*. Ed. Brian Solomon. St. Paul: Voyageur Press, 2008, pp. 91–92.

Page 50, line 5: *Nothing Like It in the World: The Men Who Built the Transcontinental Railroad, 1863–1869*, p. 366.

Page 50, line 24: Bob Zeller. E-mail interview. 1 Oct. 2014.

Page 51, line 6: Ibid.

Page 54, caption: *The Great West Illustrated in a Series of Photographic Views Across the Continent Taken Along the Line of the Union Pacific Railroad, West from Omaha*, plate 32.

Page 54, col. 2, line 2: *Photography and the Old West*, p. 135.

Page 55, line 18: *Westward to Promontory: Building the Union Pacific Across the Plains and Mountains*, p. 17.

Select Bibliography

Ambrose, Stephen E. *Nothing Like It in the World: The Men Who Built the Transcontinental Railroad, 1863–1869*. New York: Simon and Schuster, 2000.

Bain, David H. *Empire Express: Building the First Transcontinental Railroad*. New York: Viking, 1999.

Brown, Dee. *Hear that Lonesome Whistle Blow: Railroads in the West*. New York: Holt, Rinehart and Winston, 1977.

Combs, Barry B. *Westward to Promontory: Building the Union Pacific Across the Plains and Mountains*. Palo Alto, Calif.: American West Pub. Co., 1969.

Current, Karen. *Photography and the Old West*. New York: H.N. Abrams, 1978.

Dodge, Grenville M. *How We Built the Pacific Union Railway And Other Railway Papers and Addresses*. Council Bluffs, Iowa: Monarch Printing Co., 1910.

Griswold, Wesley S. *A Work of Giants: Building the First Transcontinental Railroad*. New York: McGraw-Hill, 1962.

Howard, Robert W. *The Great Iron Trail: The Story of the First Transcontinental Railroad*. New York: Putnam, 1962.

James, Edwin. *Account of an Expedition from Pittsburgh to the Rocky Mountains, Performed in the Years 1819, 1820*. Vol. 3. London: Longman, Hurst, Rees, Orme, and Brown, 1823. http://content.wisconsinhistory.org/cdm/compoundobject/collection/aj/id/17659/show/17309

Klein, Maury. *Union Pacific*. Minneapolis: University of Minnesota Press, 2006.

Naef, Weston, and James N. Wood. *Era of Exploration: The Rise of Landscape Photography in the American West, 1860–1885*. New York: New York Graphic Society, 1975.

Russell, Andrew J. *The Great West Illustrated in a Series of Photographic Views Across the Continent Taken Along the Line of the Union Pacific Railroad, West from Omaha*. New York: Union Pacific Railroad Company, 1869. http://brbl-dl.library.yale.edu/pdfgen/exportPDF.php?bibid=2006876&solrid=3434854

Russell, Andrew J. *Russell's Civil War Photographs: 116 Historic Prints*. New York: Dover Publications, 1982.

Sandweiss, Martha A. *Print the Legend: Photography and the American West*. New Haven: Yale University Press, 2002.

Stewart, John J. *The Iron Trail to the Golden Spike*. Salt Lake City: Deseret Book Co., 1996.

Vance, James E. *The North American Railroad: Its Origin, Evolution, and Geography*. Baltimore: Johns Hopkins University Press, 1995.

Walther, Susan D. *The Landscape Photographs of Alexander Gardner and Andrew Joseph Russell*. Doctoral Dissertation, Brown University, 1983.

White, Richard. *Railroaded: The Transcontinentals and the Making of Modern America*. New York: W.W. Norton and Co., 2011.

Williams, Susan E. "Richmond Again Taken: Reappraising the Brady Legend through Photographs by A.J. Russell." *Virginia Magazine of History and Biography*, Vol. 110, No. 4, 2002, pp. 437–460. http://web.b.ebscohost.com.proxy.elm4you.org/ehost/detail?vid=12&sid=346b6253-d3ba-4051-9ffc-b54406d62361%40sessionmgr198&hid=121&bdata=JnNpdGU9ZWhvc3QtbGl2ZQ%3d%3d#db=aph&AN=10134580

Williams, Susan E. "The Truth Be Told: The Union Pacific Railroad Photographs of Andrew J. Russell." *View Camera*, January-February 1996, pp. 36-43.

Zeller, Bob. *The Blue and Gray in Black and White: A History of Civil War Photography*. Westport, Conn.: Praeger, 2005.

Index

About the Author

Historian and award-winning author Don Nardo has written many books for young people, including studies of the Civil War, Mexican-American War, Native American culture and issues, and other aspects of the United States in the 19th century. In addition, he specializes in ancient history. Nardo, who also composes and arranges orchestral music, lives with his wife, Christine, in Massachusetts.